D1176223

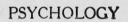

PSYCHOLOGY

THE BRITANNICA HOME UNIVERSITY

First Series

THE BRITANNICA HOME UNIVERSITY

PSYCHOLOGY

By Twenty-seven Authorities, from their Articles
in the Encyclopædia Britannica

.

THE
ENCYCLOPÆDIA BRITANNICA CO. LTD.
LONDON AND NEW YORK

CONTENTS

LIST OF AUTHORITIES

on whose articles in the

ENCYCLOPÆDIA BRITANNICA

this course is based

JAMES WARD, M.A., LL.D., Cambridge, Professor of Mental Philosophy at University 1897, Gifford Lecturer at Aberdeen 1895–7, and at St. Andrews 1908–10. Author of various works on philosophy and psychology.

ANDREW LANG, LL.D., famous British man of letters. Authority on literature, folklore, and psychical research (d. 1912).

F. C. SCOTT SCHILLER, M.A., D.Sc., Fellow and Tutor of Corpus Christi College, Oxford. President of the Society for Psychical Research.

ERIC D. MACNAMARA, M.A., M.D., F.R.C.P., Lecturer in Psychological Medicine in the Charing Cross Hospital Medical School.

W. McDOUGALL, M.A., Professor of Psychology, Harvard University, (since 1920). Formerly Wilde Reader in Mental Philosophy at the University of Oxford.

G. C. ROBERTSON, M.A., well-known Scottish philosopher and psychologist. Professor of Mental Philosophy and Logic at University College, London, 1866–92 (d. 1892).

R. ADAMSON, M.A., LL.D., well-known Scottish philosopher. Professor of Logic at Glasgow University 1895–1902 (d. 1902). Author of various works on philosophy.

T. CASE, M.A., President of Corpus Christi College, Oxford. Formerly Waynflete Professor of Moral and Metaphysical Philosophy in the University of Oxford and Fellow of Magdalen College.

A. CAMPBELL FRASER, LL.D., well-known Scottish philosopher. Late Professor of Logic and Metaphysics, Edinburgh University (d. 1914).

J. H. MUIRHEAD, M.A., LL.D., Professor of Philosophy in the University of Birmingham.

THE REV. LEWIS CAMPBELL, D.C.L., LL.D., Professor of Greek, and Gifford Lecturer at St. Andrews University 1863–94 (d. 1908).

W. R. SORLEY, M.A., Litt.D., LL.D., Professor of Moral Philosophy in the University of Cambridge.

J. SULLY, LL.D., Grote Professor of the Philosophy of Mind Logic, University College, London, 1892–1903.

H. M. BLUNT, M.A., Student, Tutor, and Librarian, Christ Church, Oxford.

H. SIDGWICK, LL.D., late Professor of Moral Philosophy in the University of Cambridge (d. 1900).

ELEANOR M. SIDGWICK (Mrs. Henry Sidgwick), D.Litt., LL.D., Principal of Newnham College, Cambridge, 1892–1910. Hon. Secretary to the Society for Psychical Research.

H. H. WILLIAMS, M.A., Fellow, Tutor, and Lecturer in Philosophy, Hertford College, Oxford.

A. S. PRINGLE-PATTISON, M.A., LL.D., D.C.L., Professor of Logic and Metaphysics, University of Edinburgh. Gifford Lecturer in the University of Aberdeen 1911.

J. THEODORE MERZ, LL.D., Ph.D., D.C.L., author of "History of European Thought in the Nineteenth Century."

H. STURT, M.A., author of various works on philosophy.

C. L. MORGAN, D.Sc., LL.D., F.R.S., Principal of University College, Bristol, 1887–1909. Emeritus Professor of Psychology, University of Bristol.

W. MINTO, M.A., LL.D., late Professor of Logic and English at Aberdeen University (d. 1893).

THE REV. A. E. GARVIE, M.A., D.D., Principal of New College, Hampstead (London). Member of the Board of Theology and the Board of Philosophy, London University.

W. L. DAVIDSON, LL.D., Professor of Logic and Metaphysics, Aberdeen University.

J. H. FREESE, M.A., formerly Fellow of St. John's College, Cambridge.

J. M. MITCHELL, sometime Scholar of Queen's College, Oxford. Lecturer in Classics, East London College, University of London.

SIGMUND FREUD (b. 1856).

The originator of psychoanalysis, which has had a tremendous influence on the practical psychology of to-day.

INTRODUCTION

THE name Psychology, which is derived from the Greek words meaning the "*science*" of the "*mind*" or "*soul*," has been applied to various branches of study and speculation concerning the workings of the human mind. In nearly all its phases of development, psychology has been intimately bound up with other sciences. In the days of Greek and Latin scholarship those thinkers who wrote or taught psychology were, for the most part, philosophers, and as far as their works are concerned it is difficult at times to disentangle pure psychology—the science of the mind, from its broader setting of philosophy—the pursuit of wisdom. Similarly, in the early centuries of the Christian Church, psychology was studied in its relation to theological dogma. Again, after the Renaissance, when investigations into the nature of this world and of man were being pursued by thinkers of many nations, the study of psychology became inextricably bound up with that of natural science, with metaphysics—a branch of philosophy concerned with abstract principles, with epistemology—the science of knowledge, and with ethics—the science of conduct. Since modern times psychology has been put to more practical uses. Social questions are now studied in its light, and its principles are widely practised in relation to medicine and education, and are recognized even in the business world.

Modern psychology is, moreover, closely concerned with questions of religion, and one branch of it—psychical research—even touches the sphere of occultism. Thus we see that psychology is concerned with almost every department of human life, and a knowledge of it is all-important if we are rightly to understand conditions in the world to-day.

9

PSYCHOLOGY

CHAPTER I

EARLY HISTORY

THE foundations of psychology, like those of many another modern science, were laid in ancient Greece, and certain principles with regard to it were stated by some of the old Greek thinkers, and have been recognized as true all through the ages.

In the philosophical works of Plato (c. 427–347 B.C.) we are able to discover certain definite psychological concepts. His philosophy is based on the fundamental distinction between the world of ideas and the world of phenomena (i.e. things perceived). The bodily senses are concerned with the latter, and perish with the body itself. The soul or mind (the same Greek word is used for both) is, however, part of the eternal reality. Its essential function is reason, and its power of reasoning is not acquired through the senses, but exists as part of its very nature, having been implanted in some previous state of existence. Plato's ideas on these subjects are found notably in " Timæus," " Phædo," " Phædrus," and the " Republic." Book VII of the " Republic " refers to education, and in it a more detailed treatment of psychology is found.

If Plato sought ultimate reality in the realm of ideas, the genius of his distinguished pupil Aristotle (384–322 B.C.) was devoted rather to the study of the world around him, and he attributes to the individual phenomena of the material universe the same reality which Plato maintains is only possessed by their universal prototypes in the eternal world of ideas.

PLATO (427–347 B.C.)

One of the earliest philosophers, who gave to the world of "ideas" pre-eminence over the world of matter.

He left writings on many subjects, including natural history, philosophy, economics, ethics, art, and psychology. This last subject is treated (notably in his " De Memoria ") in a strictly logical manner. He considers memory to be due to the association of ideas, one experience when present in the mind naturally recalling others. Besides this treatise on pure psychology, Aristotle also touched on it indirectly when writing on other subjects, as, for instance, ethics and art. As regards the latter he maintained that the function of the higher arts was to appeal to people's emotion—that the aim of tragedy in particular was to purify their passions by inspiring pity and terror. (*See* " Poetics," 1449, b. 24.)

For several centuries after Aristotle there was no advance in the treatment of psychology. The next writer on that subject whom we need consider was St. Augustine of Hippo (A.D. 354–430), one of the

ARISTOTLE (384–322 B.C.)

The ancient Greek philosopher, whose teachings on Philosophy and Æsthetics have formed the groundwork of modern research on these subjects.

Fathers of the Latin Church, author of the well-known " Confessions " and of other ecclesiastical writings. His view of human nature and consequent treatment of psychology are considerably biased in favour of Christian dogma, and he devotes much effort to reconciling the idea of free will with the doctrine of Divine Grace (i.e. that man was fundamentally evil, and could only find salvation through the mercy of the Creator), evolving at last the doctrine of Predestination as a compromise between these two views. As regards his conception of purely mental processes, St. Augustine is to some extent indebted to Aristotle. In his views on memory, however, he lays more emphasis on the association of ideas by *contiguity*, i.e. we recollect an experience by calling up different " parts " of it, which in their turn recall others until the complete picture is formed.

During the Middle Ages the study of psychology was pursued to some extent by the Schoolmen, though mainly in its relation to theology and religious experience. Thus Thomas Aquinas (*c.* 1227–1274), one of the greatest representatives of scholasticism, and himself familiar with the works of Plato and Aristotle, devoted the second part of his " Summa Theologiæ " to a discussion of the nature of man, dealing with various ethical and psychological questions. As regards the freedom of the will, Thomas Aquinas takes up the view of moderate determinism, namely that the will—in human beings as also in the Divine nature— is subject to *reason*, and that reason determines the action of the will in accordance with its own conception of what is good. This theory implies the existence of an unconditioned standard of " good," a *perseitas boni*. The question of free will was one of the chief points over which Thomas Aquinas and his school (afterwards known as the *Thomists*) came into opposition to the *Scotists*, or followers of Duns Scotus (*c.* 1265–1308), who postulated an absolute freedom of the will independently of the dictates of reason. Duns Scotus maintained, moreover, that there is no absolute *perseitas boni*—that things are only good because they are willed or sanctioned by God. In spite of this opposition, however, Thomism prevailed, and has become the official philosophy of the Roman Catholic Church.

ARTICLES TO BE READ

CHAPTER II

THE CARTESIAN SCHOOL

THE origins of modern psychology, like those of many other branches of modern science, may be traced to the Renaissance, the great intellectual reawakening which spread over Europe from the fifteenth to the seventeenth centuries. It was then that interest was revived in the pagan philosophers of Greece and Rome whose works had been almost forgotten in the West for the last thousand years ; and the desire for free thought was thereby aroused in contemporary scholars, who refused to be thwarted in their speculations by the authority of ecclesiastical

tradition. The right to doubt all transmitted information and to pursue a free unbiased investigation

DESCARTES (1596–1650)

The famous philosopher of the Renaissance, whose writings opened the way for
modern psychological research.

into the nature of the world and of man was claimed
and exercised by many thinkers at that time, among

others by the French philosopher René Descartes
(1596–1650).

Descartes' philosophy is of an abstract kind, and
his ideas on psychology are very much bound up
with metaphysics. His system of reasoning begins
with a complete doubt of everything except of his
own power to think, and he maintains that even in
human beings the mind is the only factor of whose
existence he can be absolutely certain. " Cogito
ergo sum "—" I think therefore I am "—is the fundamental axiom of his philosophy. By a process of
mathematical reasoning he proves to himself the
existence of God ; and he admits the existence of a
physical universe (i.e. extended matter) created by
God and governed by the laws of motion. Animal
life he considers to be purely a matter of automatic
reactions, as is also the physical life of man. This
brings us to Descartes' views on psychology, which
involve an essential dualism in the nature of man,
i.e. his mind—which is a purely human faculty, on
the one hand, and his physical nature—which he
shares with the rest of the animal world, on the other.
Yet the mental and physical aspects of human nature
are not wholly separate, but interact one on the other.
Their point of contact is the pineal gland, upon which
impressions from the outer world strike on the personality. The action of thought has two elements—
perception, which is passive, and volition, which is
dynamic and influences judgment. The effect of
an impression on the personality may therefore be
double. For example, some image (e.g. causing fear)

strikes upon the pineal gland, and causes the muscles to react, and automatically to prepare for flight. It is also communicated to the mind, which perceives

MALEBRANCHE (1638-1715)

A follower of Descartes, who, being a Catholic priest, tried to reconcile Cartesian philosophy with the tenets of the Church.

that there is cause for fear. The mind, however, does not react automatically, but reasons what is best to do under the circumstances—or *should* reason if the

2

will is sufficiently strong to compel it to do so. Wrong-doing is therefore the outcome of *ignorance*—i.e. of failure on the mind's part to reason, which should not occur if the *will* is strong. Descartes maintains, moreover, that an essential difference exists between ideas formed by the action of the will and through the influence of the external world, and ideas on abstract truths which are apparently formed in the mind independently of external conditions. These last he calls *innate* ideas, and it was on this point that he was strongly criticized by the English philosopher Locke.

The ideas of Descartes give rise to what is known as Cartesian philosophy, which enjoyed much popularity for about a century both in France and other countries. How this philosophy was developed by Malebranche (1638–1715) and Spinoza (1632–1677) is admirably explained in the article Cartesianism in the Encyclopædia. Spinoza made a considerable advance on the original doctrines of Descartes, and arrived at an idealism which regarded matter not as inferior to spirit but as an equal necessity in the scheme of things. He does not deny their essential duality in kind (which was one of Descartes' fundamental theories), but qualifies this theory by stating that, *ideally* considered, mind (or spirit) and matter, like God and nature, are two aspects of the same reality. He considers, moreover, that reality does not exist except in relation to the infinite, that finite things are only forms or limitations of an infinite extension of matter, and that relative ideas of good and evil (which would imply a certain independence of finite things) vanish when contemplated *sub specie æternitatis*—in the light of eternity. Similarly knowledge derived from the outer (finite) world is liable to be erroneous, and the

GOTTFRIED LEIBNITZ (1646–1716)

The German philosopher. He revised the system of the ancient Greek philosopher Democritus, who considered the universe to be a collection of monads or individual atoms.

human mind can gain no genuine knowledge unless this comes from God.

As a reaction against this universal idealism in Spinoza's philosophy there arose in Germany the metaphysical school of G. W. Leibnitz (1646–1716), who stood

essentially for the principle of individuality.   Leibnitz
revived, moreover, the system of the ancient Greek
philosopher Democritus (fifth century B.C.), whereby
the universe was conceived of as a collection of *monads*

IMMANUEL KANT (1724–1804)

The famous German philosopher.   His system draws a sharp distinction between
knowledge gained by experience and *a priori* knowledge.

or individual atoms.   Unlike Democritus, however,
who imagined these monads to be purely material,
Leibnitz considered them to be centres of spiritual
force—God himself being one of them.

Individuality and experience were, indeed, the watchwords of the eighteenth century, both in metaphysics and psychology.

As regards metaphysics, however, this point of view was to a large extent refuted in the works of Immanuel Kant (1724–1804). After a long process of reflection on the nature and possibility of knowledge, Kant arrived at the conclusion that empirical (i.e. gained by experience), or *a posteriori*, knowledge is merely a synthesis of sense experiences, and therefore unreliable, but that within every individual there exists the possibility of *a priori* knowledge, which relates to abstract truth. The former type of knowledge is gained through the understanding, the latter through reason. Among Kant's numerous writings, those which contain the most concise statements of his metaphysical views are the Dissertation " De mundi sensibilis et intelligibilis forma et principiis " (1770), and the " Kritik der reinen Vernunft "—" Critique of Pure Reason " (1781).

ARTICLES TO BE READ

CHAPTER III

ASSOCIATION PSYCHOLOGY

WE will now turn from the abstract psychology of the Cartesian school to a more concrete kind which developed as a reaction against it. This is known as Association psychology, and is concerned with the process by which ideas rise to consciousness, contending that they do so through the law of mental association. According to this law an idea comes into the mind as the logical sequence of others already there, one idea suggesting another through similarity, contrast, the law of cause and effect, or some other logical factor. Association psychology thus reduces thinking from a metaphysical abstraction to a mechanical process of the mind, and contends, moreover, that knowledge is essentially a matter of experience, not of intuition or innate ideas. A tendency towards the association point of view may be noted in some of the writings of Aristotle (though primarily in relation to memory), also in those of St. Augustine, and of Luis Vives (1492–1540), a Spanish commentator on Aristotle.

The doctrine in modern times belongs, however, essentially to the British school of psychology, and was promulgated from the seventeenth to the nineteenth centuries by a succession of English and Scottish thinkers.

The first of these thinkers is Thomas Hobbes (1588–1679), whose principal works are " Human Nature " (1650) and " Leviathan " (1651). He was, however, little more than the forerunner of associationism, though he inaugurated that type of psychology out of which it naturally evolved. His own contribution to psychology lay in an attempt to establish a definite

THOMAS HOBBES (1588-1679)

The author of "Leviathan," who was one of the forerunners of the British School of Psychology.

relation between mental activity and the experience of the senses, thus treating all thoughts and ideas as due to material sensation.

John Locke (1632-1704), whose " Essay concerning Human Understanding " (1690) was written to oppose the doctrine of innate ideas characteristic of the Cartesian school, was the first of these writers actually to use the phrase " association of ideas." It appears as the title of a supplementary chapter added to the fourth edition of his " Essay." He conceives of this association more, however, as a factor accounting for the mental peculiarities of individuals rather than as a general psychological principle. By the term " idea " Locke refers to any kind of mental experience, and distinguishes, moreover, between ideas of " sensation " and ideas of " reflection." Some ideas acquired originally through the senses may, according to him, be changed by a faculty which he calls reflection into other forms ; whilst certain ideas may be derived merely through this faculty, such as memories, reasoning, etc.

We now pass on to George Berkeley (1685–1753), who though an idealist in his metaphysical views, lays much emphasis on the empirical aspect of psychology, i.e. the importance of experience. He insists, moreover, on the principle of mental association—a suggestion, as he calls it, stating it as follows : " That one idea may suggest another to the mind it will suffice that they have been observed to go together without any demonstration of the necessity of their coexistence." (See " The New Theory of Vision," section 25.) In his analysis of mental processes Berkeley introduced a new factor, which was of considerable value in regard to the later development of psychology, namely the theory of space perception. It occurred to him that distance and depth were not perceived in the same manner as physical sensations, but necessitated some further mental faculty, and this idea of his gave rise subsequently to a deeper analysis into experience of all kinds.

In his two works " Enquiry concerning Human Understanding " and " Treatise of Human Nature," David Hume (1711–1776) continued in Berkeley's trend of thought although reverting to Locke's broader mode of inquiry. He was the first thinker since Aristotle to present a well-defined classification of the types of mental association. Ideas, he states, succeed one another as the result of resemblance, contiguity in time or space, or of cause and effect, and considers that this enumeration will explain all instances of mental association. (*See* " Enquiry concerning Human Understanding," section 3.) He displayed originality, however, when he referred to such association as a " kind of attraction which in the mental world will be found to have as extraordinary effects as in the natural, and to show itself in as many and as various forms." (*See* " Treatise of Human Nature," Book I, part 1, section 4.)

David Hartley (1705–1757) made some important contributions to the development of association psychology. Being a physician he was concerned with the physical as well as the mental aspects of human nature, and he sought to establish a connexion between the action of the nerves and that of the mind. He rejects, however, the materialistic view of making the mind directly dependent on the nerves, and advances a theory of vibrations to account for the parallel activity of the two. Hartley achieved, moreover, a very thorough analysis of the workings of the mind, and has left us, in his " Observations," a clearly stated conception of the law of association, which he

JOHN LOCKE (1632–1704)

His " Essay concerning Human Understanding " was an epoch-making work in the development of British Psychology.

regards as the fundamental principle of psychology itself. It was through his work that British associationism was definitely crystallized into a school.

Among the followers of Hartley in psychological research we may mention Thomas Brown (1778–1820), a representative of the Scottish school of psychology. Although his views on the principles of mental association—for which he uses Hobbes's term, suggestion, agree in general with those of Hartley, he puts forward certain original ideas with regard to its application. In particular he does not admit of the connexion between mental activity and the physical side of human nature, and attempts, on the contrary, to make the association theory apply to intuitional psychology. His method of analysis is essentially an introspective one, and this is the reason why he emphasizes the *succession* and not the union of ideas as the result of association—for in our conscious experience succession only can be detected.

We now pass to a later period of associationism, when psychologists were no longer groping after definitions and principles but could take these for granted, build on them, and strike out new paths for their own.

To this later period belongs James Mill (1773–1836), whose " Analysis of the Phenomena of the Human Mind " (1829) is the standard work on nineteenth-century associationism. His method of analysis is introspective like that of Brown, though the conclusions at which he arrives are somewhat different. He regards the process of association not so much as a succession but rather as a welding together of mental experiences. One peculiar feature in his system is the treatment of belief, which he regards as indissoluble association. His son John Stuart Mill (1806–1873), though better known for his works on logic and political economy, made some important contributions to psychology. His views on this subject are set out in his annotation of his father's "Analysis of the Phenomena of the Human Mind," and in the chapter on the Laws of Mind in Book VI of his own "Logic" (1843), also in his "Examination of Sir William Hamilton's Philosophy" (1865). His ideas on psychology agree in the main with those of the elder Mill, though he differs on certain matters. Being of a logical type of mind he could not fail to recognize the weak points in his father's theory of associationism, as detected by Hamilton, and he tried to improve upon this theory.

We now come to Alexander Bain (1818–1903), Scottish philosopher and educationalist, whose work in psychology has been described by Professor William James as the "last word" of the older school of that science. Not only did he enlarge considerably the field of associationism by allowing of a greater variety of mental factors than did his predecessors, but he stood for the entire separation of psychology from metaphysics, emphasizing its intimate connexion with physical science. In this way he was the forerunner of the modern psychophysical research with its different branches, and he was among the first to recognize the value of psychology as applied to social conditions, children, and even animals.

Our survey of the British associationist school would not be complete without reference to George Henry Lewes (1817–1878) and Herbert Spencer (1820–1903), writers who are also distinguished in other branches of thought. Although their psychology is connected with that of the earlier associationists, they introduced

GEORGE BERKELEY (1685-1753)

Bishop of Boyne, a metaphysician and psychologist, who was one of the chief promoters of the British School of Association Psychology.

a new concept into it, namely the idea of evolution, which was also exercising a profound influence on contemporary developments in physical science.

This was the idea that man as a creature had evolved
from simpler forms of life, and that all life was still
evolving. They maintained, moreover, that the
workings of the mind were entirely dependent on
biological processes, and thus reduced psychology
definitely to a materialistic level. As a reaction against
the extremely introspective methods of analysis adhered
to by most of the earlier psychologists, Lewes and
Spencer were interested more in the outward mani-
festations of psychology—the observance of conduct.
This last tendency gave rise to a new branch of psychology known as *behaviourism*, which is concerned
with outward reactions, and includes in its scope animal
(or comparative) as well as human psychology.

As regards the development of association psychology in France, a few names deserve special mention.

The first outstanding representative of the French
school was Etienne de Condillac (1715–1780). Though
his general trend of philosophic thought was considerably influenced by that of Locke, his conceptions
of psychology were entirely distinct from those of
the English writers of his time.

We should also notice Charles Bonnet (1720–1793),
a Swiss by origin, who published his " Essai de Psychologie " in 1740, and his " Essai analytique sur
les Facultés de l'Ame " in 1760. Claude Adrien
Helvétius (1715–1771), whose psychological doctrines
were entirely empirical, is important chiefly through
his influence on the younger school of thinkers. His
immediate followers formed a group known as *ideal-
ogues* or idealogists, and the development of French

psychology in their hands may be compared to that of English psychology under the two Mills and Bain.

French association psychology of the nineteenth century is represented chiefly by Hippolyte Adolphe Taine (1828–1893), who is perhaps better known as a historian and literary critic. His psychological work " De l'Intelligence " appeared in 1870.

The German movement in empirical psychology during the eighteenth and nineteenth centuries is represented by Johann Friedrich Herbart (1776–1841), who was pre-eminently an educational reformer, and by Friedrich Eduard Beneke (1798–1854), whose work shows close relationship with the contemporary associationist schools. As regards the later German movement in experimental psychology, the most outstanding names are those of Johannes Peter Müller (1801–1858), Ernst Heinrich Weber (1795–1878), and Hermann Lotze (1817–1881), whose " Medicinische Psychologie " appeared in 1852. The work of these three led the way to the more recent psychophysical research of Gustav Theodor Fechner (1801–1887) and Wilhelm Max Wundt (1832–1920).

DAVID HARTLEY (1705-1757)

His work first crystallized British Associationism into a school.

ARTICLES TO BE READ

Association Psychology :

ASSOCIATION OF IDEAS	Vol. 2, p..784
T. HOBBES	Vol. 13, p. 545
J. LOCKE (SECTION—PHILOSOPHY)	Vol. 16, pp. 849–851
G. BERKELEY	Vol. 3, p. 779
D. HUME (SECTION—PHILOSOPHY)	Vol. 13, pp. 879–882
D. HARTLEY	Vol. 13, p. 35
D. STEWART	Vol. 25, p. 913
T. BROWN	Vol. 4, p. 662b, c
JAMES MILL	Vol. 18, p. 453
J. S. MILL	Vol. 18, p. 454
A. BAIN	Vol. 3, p. 221
G. H. LEWES	Vol. 16, p. 520
H. SPENCER	Vol. 25, p. 634
E. B. DE CONDILLAC	Vol. 6, p. 849
P. J. G. CABANIS	Vol. 4, p. 913
H. A. TAINE	Vol. 26, p. 360
PHILOSOPHY	Vol. 21, pp. 441c–443
J. F. HERBART	Vol. 13, p. 335
F. E. BENEKE	Vol. 3, p. 726
G. T. FECHNER	Vol. 10, p. 231
R. H. LOTZE	Vol. 17, p. 23
E. MACH	Vol. 18, p. 232 ; Vol. 31, p. 818
W. M. WUNDT	Vol. 28, p. 855 ; Vol. 32, p. 1089
W. JAMES	Vol. 15, p. 144c–d
H. MÜNSTERBERG	Vol. 19, p. 12 ; Vol. 31, p. 1043
PSYCHOPHYSICS	Vol. 22, p. 604
WEBER'S LAW	Vol. 28, p. 458

The Bibliography given at the end of the article Association of Ideas in Vol. 2 of the *Encyclopædia Britannica* should be noted by students wishing to pursue this subject further. A useful addition to this bibliography will be found in "A History of the Association Psychology," by Howard C. Warren, Stuart Professor of Psychology, Princeton University (Lond., 1921), to which the compiler is much indebted for the historical sequence in the foregoing chapter.

CHAPTER IV
MODERN CONCEPTIONS
RECAPITULATION

WE have now traced the history of psychology down to the close of the nineteenth century ; and it would be well to pause and consider the conclusions actually reached by psychological research at this period. If we turn to the article Psychology, by Professor James Ward, in Vol. 22 of the *Encyclopædia Britannica*, we shall find an interesting and detailed treatise on the different mental states and processes, including the theories accepted on these subjects, by the most advanced thinkers in academic circles. Frequent reference will, moreover, be found in the article to the older psychologists already mentioned in this history. The Encyclopædia also contains numerous subsidiary articles on different psychological ideas and conceptions, which a more advanced student may wish to follow up.

The article Psychology (Vol. 22, p. 547 and following) deals with the subject from a strictly practical point of view. Psychology, it maintains, is a matter of mental *experience*, and we must assume that the conscious personality (or Ego) exists, and that there is, moreover, an objective world (or *continuum* of time and space) to which it can react. Mental experience may be divided roughly into *cognition* (or " becoming aware "), *affect* (or " feeling "), which includes the more passive mental states, and *conation* (or " mental

3

effort "), which involves the action of the will.
The different phases of cognition are described on
pp. 554–581. The most simple of these phases is
attention, without which we can become aware of
nothing. Next we come to the theory of *presentations*, or the processes by which ideas enter
our consciousness. The primary channel through
which ideas come into the mind is that of physical
sensation. We know a thing is hot because we
feel it, or that a noise is loud because we *hear* it.
From sensation we pass on to *perception*, the process
by which the mind assimilates impressions received
by the senses and forms mental images. A mental
image once formed may be recalled even in the absence
of the original object which gave rise to it. Thus,
having once seen a particular flower, we can recall
its image to our mind—colour, shape, and scent—
without seeing it again. Or we may perhaps picture
it under an aspect slightly different from what it had
in reality—for instance with a different colour. This
brings us to the subject of imagination and memory,
which are secondary forms of presentation.

Again, it will often happen that one idea or experience will recall another idea to our minds, through the
similarity or close connexion of the two. Here we
touch on the law concerning association of ideas, a
subject upon which much has been written during the
last two centuries, as we have already seen.

The fact that ideas and memories can enter the
mind in the absence of their material counterparts
leads us to suppose the existence of a region where

these images are stored, which may be described as a memory continuum—analogous, in the mental world, with the time-and-space continuum from which our material sensations are derived. This continuum is not subject to the ordinary laws of time and space—everything in it on which the attention is focused becomes " present." The images stored therein are partially accessible at will, but tend with the lapse of time to sink below the field of consciousness—in other words, to be forgotten. Once forgotten, they are no longer directly amenable to the will, but can, as a rule, only be recovered by following up the train of associations to which they are attached.

Having thus completed its survey of the simpler aspects of cognition, the article on Psychology proceeds to analyse (on pp. 581–603) the more complicated mental processes. It is shown how receptive states of mind are transformed through *emotion* into dynamic ones. Emotion (mental feeling as distinguished from physical sensation) may arise directly from sensations causing pleasure or pain, or may, in the higher mental states, arise through ideas or images which do not in themselves produce such feelings but suggest others that do. Among the more subtle types of emotion we must include intellectual feelings, i.e. certainty, doubt, interest, etc., and æsthetic pleasure. Emotion of any kind gives rise as a rule to emotional expression or *conative* action. The former is usually manifested by some sort of movement or *motor* action, either voluntary or involuntary.

Conative action, which is prompted by the desire

to prolong the emotion if agreeable or to stop it if painful, may be physical or mental. If mental, it may give rise to *intellection*, a conscious and reasoned search after means to gratify such desire—which search may involve analytical thought, discrimination, judgment, etc. As regards the development and communication of conscious thought, it should be noted that *language* is an almost indispensable factor. In pursuing analytical thought we perceive the existence of what are known as *categories*—mental concepts such as unity, likeness, difference, etc. Also the normal individual will be guided in such thinking by a certain innate logic, and will recognize the law of cause and effect, logical necessity, etc.

The mention of logical necessity brings us to an inquiry into the mental process known as belief, and postulates the " objectivity " of thought and cognition. For although emotion and desire may frequently give rise to subjective certainty in any matter, the ultimate ground for certainty lies, as a rule, outside the thinker's mind, and is to be found in the relation of the objects of thought among themselves.

From a discussion of subjects and objects in the external world we pass on to the more subtle conception of subject and object in the thinker himself, i.e. to the idea of self-consciousness and all that it involves. It will be seen that the development of intellection and self-consciousness reacts forcibly upon the emotional and active side of the personality. This reaction is manifested in *conduct* or behaviour. As regards human beings, however, another factor must be reckoned with in our estimate of conduct, namely the action of the will. This factor *appears* at any rate to be capable of counteracting or modifying the

DAVID HUME (1711-1776)

Historian and philosopher, who was the first thinker since Aristotle to present a well-defined classification of the types of mental association.

promptings of emotion and desire. Whether the will is indeed free or whether the actions of men are pre-determined has been the subject of much speculation all through the ages, and even now it is impossible for us to say. This question is still unsettled in the sphere of metaphysics as it is in that of pure psychology.

The article on Psychology ends with two sections dealing with the relation of body and mind, and with *comparative* or animal psychology. Recent psychophysical research has thrown a certain light on both these subjects, and various theories have been put forward concerning them. But we have little definite knowledge on either of them, though it seems probable that a certain *psychoneural parallelism*, or parallel action of the mind and nerves, operates in human beings, and possibly also in the more highly evolved members of the animal kingdom. It is noted, moreover, that even the lower forms of animal life react to their surroundings, though whether mechanically or not we do not know. Further information on these subjects will be found in the articles Instinct, Vol. 14, and Behaviourism, Vol. 30.

It will be noticed that reference has been made at different points in the article on Psychology to the existence of the *subconscious mind*, notably in connexion with the theory of presentations (pp. 559–560), and the memory continuum. Though treated as a hypothesis, it is stated that this idea of the subconscious mind (sometimes called *unconscious* mind) serves to explain various facts which would otherwise be unaccountable. Certain foreshadowings of this idea are, moreover, to be found in the works of some of the older psychologists, such as Leibnitz and Fechner

At the present day, however, it is no longer regarded as a hypothesis but accepted as a fact, and is indeed one of the fundamentals of contemporary psychology. The subconscious mind is conceived of as an extension of the conscious one, and as retaining all the memories and experiences which the latter has forgotten. It is beyond the scope of the will, and functions automatically. It is, however, amenable to suggestion, and if the idea be impressed on it, is capable of reasoning in its own way, and will often be of considerable assistance to the conscious mind by solving problems or recovering hidden memories. It is said to be most active during sleep, when it is no longer dominated by the conscious mind, so that on awaking the individual will often find the desired solution or memory flash into his consciousness.

The scope and extent of the subconscious mind have not yet been fully estimated. It is supposed to be in touch with certain universal life forces, which give it a creative power. Thus, ideas impressed upon it may often be translated into real fact. The subconscious mind is also said to be the channel through which the inspiration of genius finds its way into the conscious mind. The part of it concerned with inspiration, intuition, and the like is termed by some the *superconscious* mind. In its connexion with the investigations of psychical research the subconscious mind is sometimes called the *subliminal self*, an expression which became widely known through the writings of F. W. H. Myers.

The hypothesis of the subconscious mind was then one of the most vital contributions handed on by the older academic psychology to the newer school which we are about to discuss. It is true that the ideas of the older school on this subject were very scanty in comparison with our present knowledge of it, which we owe largely to the researches of Freud. Still, the idea was an all-important one, without which the work of the new school of psychology would have been well-nigh impossible.

ARTICLES TO BE READ

See also the list of articles and biographies under " Philosophy and Psychology," Vol. 29, pp. 939–940.

CHAPTER V

THE NEW PSYCHOLOGY

BY the beginning of the twentieth century a new current was discernible in the development of psychology. This was the definite recognition of the power of mind over matter, a point of view which had been coming to the fore during the last quarter of the previous century. This truth had been emphasized in various schools of thought, mostly of religious or therapeutic tendency. The Christian Science movement, which was started in America about 1866 by Mrs. Baker Eddy (1821–1910), was among the most prominent of these schools of thought, and was, moreover, founded as a definite religious sect. Christian Scientists hold as their fundamental principle the all-pervading power of mind, and maintain that material things are entirely subservient to it. They teach, moreover, that man, being an emanation of the Divine mind, is, and must be, perfect, and that all evil and sickness are delusions due to wrong thinking. They claim to be able to heal disease by the power of thought, notably by denying that disease exists, and their efforts are, in many cases, successful.

Other schools of healing by the more orthodox methods of religion, such as faith and prayer, have also arisen during the last few decades and done good and useful work. The percentage of cures achieved by these different methods, which may be directly due to supernatural agency, we will not discuss, as this lies somewhat beyond the field of psychology as we know it at present. A large proportion of them can, however, be explained as the result of *suggestion*, which is indeed the main force by which mind dominates matter. Suggestion may be described briefly as the power of the mind to create by means of realization. As we have already seen, the subconscious mind possesses a mysterious creative faculty, and is able under certain conditions to translate into fact images impressed upon it either by its own conscious mind or from without. In the former case the process is called auto-suggestion. Thus, a sick person treated by Christian Science or faith healing might, if persuaded to believe himself cured, easily become well. This is true, especially of mental or nervous disorders, though it has also been proved in cases of physical disease. How far the effects of suggestion can be hindered or counteracted by other factors is not exactly known, but as a psychological principle suggestion is now universally recognized and is indeed one of the fundamental elements of modern psychology. It can take a variety of forms, such as auto-suggestion, when exercised by an individual upon himself, and " mass " or " herd " suggestion when a large number of people are dominated by some idea or delusion. It can be used for beneficial purposes such as healing, or for detrimental ones as in the case of some kinds of *hypnotism*, where the mind and will of the person who receives the suggestion are weakened by the dominance of a stronger personality.

Hypnotism—the control of one mind by another— has been known and practised in Europe for more than a century. If rightly used it may be of considerable value in mental healing, and is resorted to at present in certain difficult cases of mental treatment, as an alternative to *psychoanalysis*. This last is the name given to a system of diagnosing mental and nervous diseases, which was discovered and made popular by the Viennese doctor Sigmund Freud (b. 1856), who in his earlier work had used hypnotism. It may be explained as follows : Mental and nervous diseases are known to be due, in many cases, to some repression, shock, or conflict in the mind of the sufferer ; and it has also been proved that the mere realization by the latter of the cause of his trouble is often enough to cure it. A difficulty arises, however, in the fact that the repression, conflict, or other cause of disease has in most cases been forgotten by the person concerned, i.e. buried in his subconscious mind. It is the work of psychoanalysis to bring it to light. This is effected by a variety of methods—sometimes by following up a train of thought in the patient's mind, ascertaining the ideas or images which he associates with certain given ideas, so as eventually to arrive by this series of associations at the hidden cause of the trouble. In the more

E. B. DE CONDILLAC (1715–1780)

The prominent French psychologist who was also one of the founders of the famous French "Encyclopédie."

difficult cases hypnotism is still resorted to instead of simple analysis, in order to give freer outlet to the contents of the subconscious mind by putting the conscious mind temporarily into abeyance. Psychoanalysis, if successfully conducted, should bring to light some repressed idea or associated group of ideas—technically known as a complex, induced probably by shock, fright, or repression, which though actually forgotten by the individual has, nevertheless, been poisoning his mental life, and probably affecting his thoughts and actions in more ways than he has imagined. Freud was originally inclined to attribute all mental and nervous disorders to complexes of a sexual nature. Later, however, he modified his views and admitted the possibility of other causes, as do the well-known Swiss doctor Jung and other contemporary psychologists. The occurrence of shell-shock during the war has, moreover, clearly shown that sex is not the only possible cause of nervous trouble. Psychoanalysis has, however, proved that the roots of such trouble lie in many cases very deeply buried, and may indeed be traced back to one or more of the primal instincts of human nature—self-preservation, sex, or the herd instinct, or possibly to a conflict between these instincts.

Thus we see that psychoanalysis has been an epoch-making discovery in the history of psychology, and greatly extended the possibilities of mental healing. It should be noted, though, that this treatment is not without its dangers, especially if attempted by an unskilled practitioner. Our knowledge of the subconscious mind is still rudimentary, and any tampering with its working or contents should be undertaken only with the greatest caution. It has, moreover, been shown by practice that the ruthless dissecting of a neurotic person's mind and the dragging to light of hidden complexes may only result in making that person more unbalanced, unless some constructive idea is given to him to take the place of these complexes and thus synthesize his mental outlook.

The instilling of constructive ideas—the rebuilding of personality—is the chief aim of the most recent psychological movement usually known as " Practical Psychology," or " Applied Psychology."

A general interest in psychology of this kind has sprung up during recent years, and there are at the present time an ever-increasing number of practitioners and students of it both in Europe and America. It appeals to average people through its intensely practical message, since it purports to help them to understand themselves and make the best of life. Although based on the accepted premises of mind-power and the use of suggestion, practical psychology is not quite like any earlier school of thought. It stands for the all-pervading power of mind in the universe and the creative power of thought. It maintains, moreover, that human minds are essentially one with the universal or Divine mind, and that, in virtue of this unity, it is possible for human beings through right thinking to use the power of mind for healing and the improvement of conditions. Practical psychology is a tremendously interesting subject, about which more is being discovered every day. Its tenets are not static but evolutionary. Unlike Christian Science, it teaches *not* that man is already perfect, but that, being one with the Creative Spirit of Life, he has within him the germ of perfection, which may be developed by right living and thinking.

Among the practical channels in which psychology is now applied, special mention should be made of education. The idea of such application is, however, by no means new, as it has long been recognized among enlightened educationists that a healthy mental outlook, or the reverse, exercises an immense influence on the intellectual and moral growth of young people. The educational systems of J. H. Pestalozzi (1746–1827), F. J. Herbart (1776–1841), and of F. W. A. Froebel (1782–1852) bear witness to the persistence of this theory. The aim of Froebel's " Kindergarten " schools, which have since his time attained great popularity both in Europe and America, is to train young children in congenial surroundings and an atmosphere of happiness so as to induce not only intellectual growth but a harmonious development of the entire personality.

During recent years, since psychology has come to be studied on scientific lines, it has been applied to education with a view to assisting mentally defective children. Among the experimental systems started with this object, that of Doctor Maria Montessori (b. 1870) deserves special mention. By carefully stimulating in them the desire for knowledge or achievement in small ways and by imposing as few restrictions on them as possible, she has succeeded in awakening the latent faculties of many a backward or defective child. Her system is, moreover, applied with success to normal children.

The application of psychology to social conditions and problems is too wide a subject to be treated in detail here.　Schemes and experiments for this purpose are increasing year by year in various departments of life, as people come to recognize the importance of mind-power as a factor for inducing health and efficiency, and to realize, moreover, that the best work is obtained from workers who are treated sympathetically —as human beings and not as mere machines.　The recognition of these psychological principles in the industrial world has given rise, during the last two decades, to what is known as welfare work.　This term is used to cover various schemes—now officially recognized both in Great Britain and the United States— organized with the object of promoting the physical and mental well-being of workers in factories and industrial concerns.　Welfare work seeks not only to make the industrial workers feel that life is worth living, but also to make them realize their own responsibility as human beings and as citizens, and to instil into them a healthy social code and a spirit of co-operation.

This spirit of co-operation, which is so necessary in the social relations of everyday life, is also the sole factor which is able to ensure harmony in the more complicated activity of the State.　This brings us to the question of psychology in its application to the State and to history, a far-reaching subject with great possibilities, about which little has up to the present been written or formulated.　It may be of interest, however, to read in this connexion the concluding section of the article *Philosophy*, Vol. 21, p. 444, in which the philosophy of the State and of history is discussed. It might almost be possible, indeed, to substitute the word " psychology " for " philosophy " in the present case, since any consideration of the nature or workings of the State reduces itself ultimately to a study of human nature. We read in this article how the question of ethics or morality has, from the earliest times, been recognized as a fundamental one in any consideration of the State, and it is indeed easy to understand that the principles of conduct which hold good in the lesser departments of life will also be true in the widest sphere of man's activities, namely the State. The writers mentioned in this article who have formulated theories on this subject—Plato, Aristotle, Lessing, and Hegel—all recognized this to be true. Also in the ideal representations of the State which Sir Thomas More has given us in his " Utopia " (1516), and J. J. Rousseau in his " Contrat Social " (1762), the principle of harmonious co-operation between individuals is one of the main factors by which the political and social structure is maintained.

Likewise the facts of history, if considered in the light of philosophy or psychology, become something more than a chance sequence of events. They show us the reaction of human nature in definite environment or conditions, and trace man's age-long struggle to become master of his circumstances. To quote Lessing's conception of it, history is the " education of the human race." There are, of course, two distinct attitudes which the student can adopt with regard to the philosophy of history ; one being the determinist

4

or materialist attitude, which considers human nature as unchanging and bound to react in a certain manner under given conditions. The other is the evolutionary point of view which allows to man a certain degree of free will and with it the power to develop and improve himself and to rise superior to his circumstances. Here, however, we infringe on the sphere of metaphysics.

As far as psychology is concerned, we may say that in order to complete its work for humanity, it must include every department of life within its survey. In social and political life it must work for the reconciliation of individual development with the interest of the whole. It should also be able to interpret the events of history as a natural and reasonable sequence, pre-determined, perhaps, to some extent, but in which man's higher faculties are ever growing and developing.

It may not be out of place to mention here that the ideal of co-operation and mutual forbearance, which has been proved to be the only satisfactory one in individual and social relations, has of recent years been applied, tentatively it is true, to international affairs. The principle of self-determination whereby certain peoples have been permitted to choose their own political allegiance has already been tried, and should, if rightly conducted, do away with a great deal of national discontent. The theory of self-determination and the conditions in which it is feasible or desirable are discussed in the article *Self-determination*, Vol. 32, p. 391. Another attempt to establish a system of " give-and-take " in international affairs may be noted in the establishment of the League of Nations. The ideals for which the League was founded and the history of similar attempts in

DR. MONTESSORI GIVING A LESSON IN TOUCHING
GEOMETRICAL INSETS.
[Photo reproduced from " The Montessori Method," by permission of the publishers, Wm. Heinemann & Co.]

the past are discussed at the outset of the article *League of Nations*, Vol. 31, pp. 735–736.

It is early yet to pronounce an opinion on the success or failure of these international experiments ; time alone can prove their efficacy. Their success or failure will depend on whether the principles on which they are based are sound and answer to the requirements of humanity as a whole.

ARTICLES TO BE READ

CHAPTER VI

PSYCHICAL RESEARCH

OUR study of psychology will scarcely be complete without a brief survey of that most interesting though debatable branch of it—psychical research. This is a broad term used to define the study of what are termed psychic phenomena, i.e. faculties and occurrences observed from time to time both in human personalities and the outer world which cannot be wholly accounted for by any known laws either of psychology or physical science, and which may in some cases be due to supernormal agency. Typical among the more widely known varieties of psychic phenomena are the faculty of second sight, possessed by certain people, and the disturbances in the so-called " haunted " houses. Although psychical research as an organized study did not exist before the nineteenth century, the phenomena which it sets out to investigate are as old as the human race itself, and have been noted at all periods and among practically all races. The fact that no real investigation of them was undertaken until modern times is not hard to explain. In ancient and mediæval days, when people possessed far less scientific knowledge than they do at present, any supernormal faculties or happenings were either regarded with super-stitious terror or else stigmatized as " witchcraft " and suppressed. By the eighteenth century, however, a reaction set in, and scepticism took the place of super-stition in the minds of educated people. The materialistic age which followed deserves, at any rate, the credit of putting an end to the official persecution of witches—at least in the more advanced countries. At the same time, however, little serious interest was taken in matters outside the physical sphere, and it was not till about the middle of the nineteenth century that psychic phenomena became the object of or-ganized study. Just at that period a keen interest was awakened in these matters, encouraged, moreover, by the vogue for spiritualism (i.e. communication with departed spirits) and " table-turning," which spread from America to Europe. A genuine desire to submit these and kindred phenomena to scientific investigation was aroused and has never since died out. In 1882 the Society for Psychical Research was founded in England, under the presidency of Henry Sidgwick, and has enrolled among its members many names of Englishmen distinguished in other branches of learning and culture, as those of F. W. H. Myers, Andrew Lang, Lord Tennyson, Lord Rayleigh, and others. This Society was later incorporated with a similar organization founded in America in 1884, and has done much persevering work in collecting and sifting evidence with regard to psychic phenomena. They have also conducted experiments, formulated theories, and published records of their work in numerous volumes of " Proceedings." One of the results of the late war was, moreover, a recrudescent interest in psychic matters, especially in the question of communicating with the dead. Numerous bereaved persons attempted, by consulting mediums and by other methods, to get into touch with their lost relatives and friends. Among them was the well-known scientist Sir Oliver Lodge. In 1916 he published a book, entitled " Raymond," describing his experiences in trying to communicate with his son who had been killed in Flanders ; the object of this book being to convince the world of the possibility of communication with the departed. Another eminent

writer who became convinced at this time of the reality
of the spirit world was Sir A. Conan Doyle, who has
made clear his point of view in " The New Revelation "
(1918) and " The Vital Message " (1919), originally

Photo by]   *[Topical.*
SIR OLIVER LODGE
Formerly President of the Society for Psychical Research, and still one of
the leaders in that field, and the author of many works on Physics, Ethics, and
Psychology.

published in England. During these years numerous
messages purporting to come from the spirits of
men killed in the war were also received by
different people by means of automatic writing, and
some have been published. Automatic writing has

also been the means of recording other messages from unknown, possibly supernatural, sources not connected with the war. Among the most remarkable of these messages are the ones published in England in Mr. Bligh Bond's " Gate of Remembrance " (1918), which proved to be of practical value, and led him to the discovery of certain architectural remains in Glastonbury Abbey.

We will now consider briefly the nature of some of the better-known types of psychic phenomena. A large section of these are manifested in human personality. There is the phenomenon called *telepathy* (from two Greek words meaning " feeling from a distance"). This includes thought-transference—the power of one individual to impress his thoughts on the mind of another, which is now a generally accepted fact, and is probably governed by some mechanism of the brain itself, as yet not understood. Telepathy is also supposed to include the ability, apparently possessed by certain people, of sending a visible image or vision of themselves to others, either consciously or unintentionally. This is said to occur usually when the sender of the vision is dying or in great trouble. The person to whom it is sent may be awake at the time, or may see it in a dream. Numerous instances of these visions have been recorded by the Society for Psychical Research, and, ruling out the cases which may be due to coincidence or the imagination of the person seeing the vision (technically known as *hallucination*), evidence tends to show that some mysterious connexion exists between these visions and impending death or trouble. Telepathy seems to be the only psychological explanation of these occurrences, though religion and occultism may offer others.

Another psychic phenomenon merely effecting human personality is that of automatic writing. It is well known that some people, if they hold a pencil or pen and remain in a passive condition, will find their hand guided by some agency apparently outside themselves, and will write on subjects of which they seem to have no previous knowledge. Sometimes they even write in a language normally unknown to them. Automatic writing has never been fully explained, though a variety of possible explanations has been suggested. Many people consider that it is due to some process in the subconscious mind whereby forgotten memories and impressions are forced to the surface and appear as new information. It is not easy, however, to make this explanation apply to every case of automatic writing ; there have indeed been instances in which a supernatural explanation seems the only probable one.

Then there is the problem of dissociated personality, a psychic phenomenon which can take a number of forms and has given rise to much speculation. It may take the form of a *trance*, when the conscious personality is thrown into a kind of sleep, and the individual will see visions or hear voices—as did many saints and mystics in the Middle Ages. Sometimes (as in the case of mediums or spiritualist séances) the person in a trance will appear to be controlled by some outside personality which speaks with their voice, and which is held, of course, by believers in spiritualism to be a disembodied spirit using this means to communicate with the earth. Other forms of dissociated personality, due to mental stress, have also been observed and are admirably described in the article on Psychical Research in Vol. 30 of the Encyclopædia. Dissociation of personality in itself is undoubtedly explicable on a psychological basis, but it remains a doubtful question how far the phenomenon of mediumship is to be ascribed to the workings of the subconscious mind, and how far the spirit hypothesis is to be admitted.

The last purely subjective psychic phenomenon which we have to consider is that of *clairvoyance*, including *clairaudience*. These two French words mean respectively " clear-seeing " and " clear-hearing," and refer to the faculty which some people possess of perceiving sights and sounds imperceptible to ordinary human beings, and of foretelling the future. This faculty is sometimes called second sight, and is said to be most common among people of Celtic descent. The true nature and cause of clairvoyance are at present unknown, but there is no reason to suppose that this faculty is not traceable to some mechanism latent in every human being, though more developed in some. It is possible that the subconscious mind has the power to project itself outside the ordinary confines of time and space, and is able in certain individuals to communicate what it perceives to the conscious mind.

We will now turn to the branch of psychical research which is concerned with the existence of discarnate spirits—living creatures with no physical bodies. This is a subject on which it is impossible to dogmatize, and it belongs more properly to occultism than to psychology. People gifted with second sight often affirm that they see these beings—referring to them probably as ghosts, fairies, nature-spirits, or angels ; and there seems no reason for rejecting their testimony as a whole. Of course, if we admit of the creative power of thought, it is easy to suggest that some of these appearances are merely thought-forms or objective mental images ; yet it scarcely seems probable that this explanation will meet every case. The thought-form hypothesis may, however, account for some of the " ghosts " in haunted houses, where abnormal sights or sounds recur frequently and are observed by many witnesses. It is said, indeed, that scenes fraught with strong emotion leave their impressions—absorbed, so to speak, by the places where they are enacted, and that under certain circumstances these impressions may be projected in visible or audible form, thus appearing as thought-forms.

Another type of " haunting" must also be mentioned, namely the somewhat unpleasant " poltergeist " phenomena. Poltergeist, a German word which means " racketing spirit," is the name given to the spirit which is supposed to be active in haunted houses where furniture is lifted, china smashed, etc., apparently through no material agency. It is needless to say that no satisfactory explanation has been discovered for these occurrences. It is generally noticed, however, that the disturbances happen when some particular person is in the house, and cease when that person leaves it. Thus, one explanation suggested is that certain people give off, quite involuntarily, an invisible non-material substance which is seized upon by some irresponsible nature-spirit (or *elemental*) and affords it sufficient material force to play its pranks. This same etheric substance, known variously as *plasma, ectoplasm,* or *bioplasm,* is also said to be the basis of the " materialization " phenomena known to spiritualists.

This brings us to our last subject for consideration, namely the possibility of conscious intercourse with the spirit world. Instances of supposed communication with spirits have occurred at all periods of history. We read of Saul consulting the witch of Endor, of the oracles of ancient Greece, the experiences of mediæval saints, the exploits of witches, etc. During recent years the whole subject has been submitted to close investigation, and frequent experiments have been made, mainly with a view to establishing proof of human survival after death. We have already referred to automatic writing, which is a means by which attempts are made to record messages from the unseen world. This method, though apparently satisfactory in some cases, is ultimately uncertain, since even a message genuinely emanating from super-human sources would be liable to misinterpretation through the workings of the recorder's own subconscious mind.

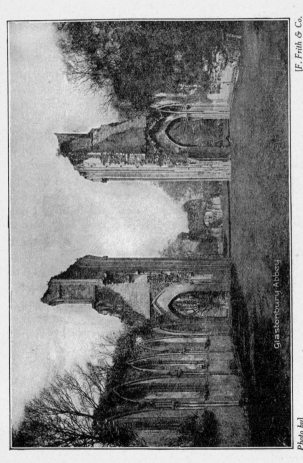

Glastonbury Abbey

Photo by] [*F. Frith & Co.*

A view of the ruins of Glastonbury Abbey where the sites of two ancient chapels have been discovered through the assistance of automatic writing.

A means of communication with spirits more frequently resorted to, especially by people who themselves possess no psychic powers, is that of consulting mediums, i.e. holding spiritualist séances. The medium (frequently a woman) passes into a trance and is then observed to speak in a voice unlike her natural one, and talk on matters which may or may not be familiar to those present. It is thought, of course, that the communicating spirit is speaking through her, and it is a curious fact that the voice will often resemble that of a dead person with whom the sitters desire to get into touch. In some cases " materialization " takes place, and the form of the spirit actually becomes visible—materialized, it is supposed, by means of the ectoplasm given off by the medium herself.

Another method of attempted communication is that of " table-turning " (with which may be classed " planchette " and similar contrivances), a method whereby the spirit is invited to spell out its message by means of rapping or mechanical devices.

Although these various experiments are of considerable interest from a scientific point of view, it must be plainly stated here that any attempt to communicate with the spirit world, by whatever method, is both uncertain and dangerous. It is uncertain because many of the results obtained may be due merely to the action of the subconscious mind or of telepathy, and dangerous because once a channel is opened for superhuman powers there seems to be little or no protection against any undesirable force which may come through. Moreover, it is, in the majority of cases, exceedingly hard to prove that what are taken at séances to be spirits of the dead may not be other, ill-conditioned, spirits impersonating them. Also the descriptions given of life in the other world may be pure fabrications, or may be evoked from, or at any rate coloured by, the subconscious minds of persons attending the séance.

In conclusion, then, we may say that as matters stand at present it is exceedingly doubtful whether satisfactory proof of human immortality can be obtained through spiritualism, or indeed through any experimental science. The whole subject belongs essentially to the sphere of religion, or is at most apprehensible by intuition of a very high order, such as few people possess.

Yet evolution is not at a standstill, and, in the face of the marvellous discoveries made recently in the field of natural science, such as wireless telephony, relativity, etc., who shall say but that correspondingly wonderful discoveries may not be made in the sphere of psychology, which shall enlarge man's intellectual capacity and his spiritual vision? And as regards the achievements of psychical research, we shall surely agree with Andrew Lang, who states at the end of his article on this subject in the *Encyclopædia Britannica* that even if no light is ever to be cast, by these means, on spiritual problems, at least the field of psychology has been thereby extended.

ARTICLES TO BE READ

See also the list of articles and biographies under " Psychical Research and Occultism," Vol. 29, p. 940, and under "Comparative Religion and Folklore," section General, Vol. 29, p. 945.